EASY GAZPACHO COOKBOOK

50 DELICIOUS GAZPACHO RECIPES

By
Chef Maggie Chow
Copyright © 2015 by Saxonberg Associates
All rights reserved

Published by
BookSumo, a division of Saxonberg Associates
http://www.booksumo.com/

INTRODUCTION

Welcome to *The Effortless Chef Series*! Thank you for taking the time to download the *Easy Gazpacho Cookbook*. Come take a journey with me into the delights of easy cooking. The point of this cookbook and all my cookbooks is to exemplify the effortless nature of cooking simply.

In this book we focus on Gazpacho. You will find that even though the recipes are simple, the taste of the dishes is quite amazing.

So will you join me in an adventure of simple cooking? If the answer is yes (and I hope it is) please consult the table of contents to find the dishes you are most interested in. Once you are ready jump right in and start cooking.

— Chef Maggie Chow

TABLE OF CONTENTS

Introduction 2

Table of Contents 3

Any Issues? Contact Me 7

Legal Notes 8

Common Abbreviations 9

Chapter 1: Easy Gazpacho Recipes 10

    West Coast Gazpacho 10

    Roman Gazpacho 13

    Sourdough Gazpacho 16

    Minty Gazpacho 19

    Two Grapes and Sherry Gazpacho 22

    Spaghetti Gazpacho 26

    Winter Solstice Gazpacho 29

    Gazpacho Medley 31

Ginger Gazpacho	34
Hot Gazpacho	37
South American Gazpacho	40
Garlic Crouton Gazpacho	43
Classical Gazpacho	46
Verde Gazpacho	48
Artisan Gazpacho	50
Countryside Gazpacho	52
Balsamic Gazpacho	55
Avocado and Garlic Gazpacho	57
Southern Gazpacho	59
Sunrise Gazpacho	61
Lime Gazpacho	64
Parsley Gazpacho	66
Maggie's Favorite Gazpacho	69
Orange and Watermelon Gazpacho	71
Hawaiian Gazpacho	74

- Gazpacho from Spain ... 77
- Jalapeno Gazpacho ... 79
- Summer Solstice Gazpacho ... 82
- Crab Gazpacho ... 85
- Western European Gazpacho ... 87
- Latin Gazpacho ... 89
- New World Ceviche ... 91
- Gazpacho Appetizer ... 94
- Sherry Gazpacho ... 96
- Gazpacho Chiller ... 98
- Manhattan Gazpacho ... 100
- Green Spanish Gazpacho ... 102
- Pasta Gazpacho ... 105
- Ripe Gazpacho ... 108
- Mexican Gazpacho ... 111
- Strawberry Pineapple Gazpacho ... 114
- East Coast Gazpacho ... 116

Little Tomato Gazpacho 119

French Style Gazpacho 122

Cha-Cha Gazpacho 125

Louisiana Gazpacho 127

Maiz Gazpacho 129

THANKS FOR READING! NOW LET'S TRY SOME **SUSHI** AND **DUMP DINNERS** 131

Come On 133

Let's Be Friends :) 133

Can I Ask A Favour? 134

Interested in Other Easy Cookbooks? 135

ANY ISSUES? CONTACT ME

If you find that something important to you is missing from this book please contact me at maggie@booksumo.com.

I will try my best to re-publish a revised copy taking your feedback into consideration and let you know when the book has been revised with you in mind.

:)

— Chef Maggie Chow

Legal Notes

ALL RIGHTS RESERVED. NO PART OF THIS BOOK MAY BE REPRODUCED OR TRANSMITTED IN ANY FORM OR BY ANY MEANS. PHOTOCOPYING, POSTING ONLINE, AND / OR DIGITAL COPYING IS STRICTLY PROHIBITED UNLESS WRITTEN PERMISSION IS GRANTED BY THE BOOK'S PUBLISHING COMPANY. LIMITED USE OF THE BOOK'S TEXT IS PERMITTED FOR USE IN REVIEWS WRITTEN FOR THE PUBLIC AND/OR PUBLIC DOMAIN.

Common Abbreviations

cup(s)	C.
tablespoon	tbsp
teaspoon	tsp
ounce	oz.
pound	lb

*All units used are standard American measurements

Chapter 1: Easy Gazpacho Recipes

West Coast Gazpacho

Ingredients

- 2 C. yellow pear tomatoes, sliced in half
- 2 yellow bell peppers, seeds removed and diced
- 1 red bell pepper, seeds removed and diced
- 1 cucumber, peeled, seeds removed and diced
- 1 bunch green onion, chopped
- 3 cloves garlic, diced
- 1 bunch cilantro, destemmed and finely chopped
- 1 jalapeno, seeds removed and diced
- 2/3 C. olive oil
- 3 tbsps white wine vinegar
- 3 tbsps finely chopped fresh chives
- salt, to taste
- fresh coarse ground black pepper, to taste

Directions

- Get a bowl, mix: jalapeno, tomatoes, cilantro, pepper, garlic, onions, and cucumbers.
- Get a 2nd bowl, combine: herbs, olive oil, and white vinegar.
- Stir the mix then add in some pepper and salt.
- Combine both bowls and let the gazpacho for 1 hr, covered in the fridge.
- Enjoy.

Amount per serving: 4

Timing Information:

| Preparation | 15 mins |
| Total Time | 15 mins |

Nutritional Information:

Calories	389.3
Fat	36.7g
Cholesterol	0.0mg
Sodium	29.4mg
Carbohydrates	16.0g
Protein	3.3g

* Percent Daily Values are based on a 2,000 calorie diet.

Roman Gazpacho

Ingredients

- 1 1/2 lbs ripe tomatoes, seeded, cut into 2 inch pieces
- 1 large cucumber, peeled, halved lengthwise, seeded, and sliced into 1/2 inch slices
- 1 red bell pepper, cut into 1 inch pieces
- 1 small red onion, coarsely chopped
- 2 cloves garlic, diced
- 1 1/2 C. tomato juice
- 1/3 C. balsamic vinegar
- 1/2 tsp salt
- 1/4 tsp red pepper flakes
- 1/3 C. chopped fresh basil, for garnish

Directions

- Add the following to the bowl of a food processor: garlic, tomatoes, onion, bell peppers, and cucumbers.
- Chop the veggies then combine in the pepper flakes, tomato juice, salt, and vinegar.
- Continue to combine the mix a few more times.

- Then pour everything into a bowl and place a covering of plastic on the bowl.
- Put everything in the fridge for 8 hrs.
- Add in some more pepper and salt and divide the mix between serving bowls.
- Top each serving with some basil.
- Enjoy.

Amount per serving: 6

Timing Information:

| Preparation | 25 mins |
| Total Time | 25 mins |

Nutritional Information:

Calories	63.8
Fat	0.4g
Cholesterol	0.0mg
Sodium	368.6mg
Carbohydrates	13.9g
Protein	2.3g

* Percent Daily Values are based on a 2,000 calorie diet.

Sourdough Gazpacho

Ingredients

- 2 tbsps extra virgin olive oil
- 3 large garlic cloves, diced
- 6 large ripe tomatoes, peeled and chopped
- 1 yellow bell pepper, chopped
- 1 yellow onion, peeled and chopped
- 1 large cucumber, peeled and chopped
- 6 tbsps white wine vinegar
- 1 slice sourdough bread, crusts removed, soaked in water and squeezed dry
- 1 tsp salt
- 1/2 tsp fresh ground pepper
- 6 drops Tabasco sauce, to taste
- 1/2 C. grape tomatoes, quartered
- 1/2 C. yellow bell pepper, chopped
- 1/2 C. cucumber, peeled and chopped
- 1/2 C. scallion, chopped

Directions

- Begin to stir fry your garlic in olive oil for 2 mins then shut the heat.

- Get a bowl, combine: garlic and oil, tomatoes, bread, yellow pepper, vinegar, cucumbers, and onions.
- Add the mix to the bowl of a food processor and begin to puree everything.
- Once the mix is smooth place everything in a bowl and stir in some tabasco, pepper, and salt.
- Place a covering of plastic on the bowl and put everything in the fridge for 60 mins.
- Dice the following veggies as the gazpacho chills: grape tomatoes, bell peppers, cucumbers, and scallions.
- Divide the chopped veggies between the gazpacho when serving everything.
- Enjoy.

Amount per serving: 6

Timing Information:

| Preparation | 15 mins |
| Total Time | 15 mins |

Nutritional Information:

Calories	135.1
Fat	5.4g
Cholesterol	0.0mg
Sodium	469.3mg
Carbohydrates	20.5g
Protein	3.8g

* Percent Daily Values are based on a 2,000 calorie diet.

Minty Gazpacho

Ingredients

- 2 thick slices onions
- 1 large beet, roasted and peeled
- 6 oz. cucumbers, peeled and coarsely chopped
- 2 lbs ripe tomatoes, quartered
- 2 sticks celery, coarsely chopped
- 2 large garlic cloves, halved, green germs removed
- 2 tbsps sherry wine vinegar, plus a little extra for the onion
- 3 tbsps extra virgin olive oil
- salt
- 1/2-1 C. ice water
- 1/2 C. diced cucumber
- slivered fresh mint leaves

Directions

- Let your onions sit submerged in water then add in a bit of vinegar.
- Leave the onions to stand for 10 mins.
- Then slice the onions.

- Add the following to the bowl of a food processor and puree them: onions, beets, cucumbers, tomatoes, celery, garlic, wine vinegar, olive oil.
- Puree the mix for 3 mins then place everything into a bowl.
- Place a covering of plastic on the bowl and put everything in the fridge 3 hrs.
- Enjoy.

Amount per serving: 6

Timing Information:

| Preparation | 10 mins |
| Total Time | 2 hrs 10 mins |

Nutritional Information:

Calories	114.7
Fat	7.1g
Cholesterol	0.0mg
Sodium	27.7mg
Carbohydrates	12.2g
Protein	2.2g

* Percent Daily Values are based on a 2,000 calorie diet.

Two Grapes and Sherry Gazpacho

Ingredients

- 3 large garlic cloves
- 2 C. diced stale bread, crusts removed
- 2 C. peeled fried and salted almonds
- 1 C. white seedless grapes, halved
- 1 C. red seedless grapes, halved
- salt
- 1 1/2 C. extra virgin olive oil
- 1 1/2-2 tbsps sherry wine vinegar
- extra virgin olive oil, as needed
- 1/4 C. diced bread
- salt
- 1/2 C. mixed red and white seedless grapes, cut into small dice
- 1/4 C. peeled fried and salted almonds
- 1 scallion, thinly sliced diagonally
- almond oil or extra virgin olive oil, for drizzling
- sherry wine vinegar, as needed

Directions

- Get your pieces of garlic boiling in water for 2 mins then remove all the liquids and place the garlic in a bowl, in a the fridge.
- Place your bread in bowl with water as well and let the bread sit submerged for 12 mins.
- Now drain the water from the bread and squeeze the bread with your hands to remove more liquids.
- Place the following in the bowl of a food processor: pieces of garlic, almonds, bread, and grapes.
- Add some salt and puree the mix.
- Get 1 C. of cold water and another with olive oil then gradually pour in both liquids into the puree with a slow speed.
- Now combine in 1.5 tbsps of vinegar and some more salt as well.
- Place the gazpacho in a bowl and place a covering of plastic on the bowl.
- Put everything in the fridge for 3 hrs.
- Now set your oven to 400 degrees before doing anything else.
- Coat your pieces of bread with olive oil and salt then place everything into a casserole dish.
- Cook the bread in the oven for 9 mins then place them in a bowl with the scallions, almonds, and grapes.
- Add in some pepper, salt, some olive oil, and some vinegar.

- Divide your gazpacho between serving dishes and top each dish with some of the scallion mix. Enjoy.

Amount per serving: 4

Timing Information:

Preparation	5 mins
Total Time	25 mins

Nutritional Information:

Calories	1306.0
Fat	122.8g
Cholesterol	10.0mg
Sodium	401.9mg
Carbohydrates	44.2g
Protein	19.6g

* Percent Daily Values are based on a 2,000 calorie diet.

Spaghetti Gazpacho

Ingredients

- 6 oz. spaghetti, uncooked
- vegetable oil cooking spray
- 1 C. broccoli floret
- 1 C. carrot, thinly sliced
- 1 C. zucchini, sliced
- 1/4 C. onion, sliced
- 1 small yellow sweet pepper, julienned
- 1/2 C. cucumber, sliced
- 1/2 C. fresh mushrooms, sliced
- 1 small tomatoes, cut into 8 wedges
- 2 tbsps dry vermouth
- 6 tbsps grated parmesan cheese
- 1 tbsp fresh parsley, diced
- 1/4 tsp sweet red pepper flakes

Directions

- Get your pasta boiling in water and salt for 9 mins then remove all the liquids.
- Begin to stir fry your broccoli, carrots, zucchini, and onions, in a frying pan with nonstick spray for 6 mins then combine in the mushrooms, cucumbers, and yellow pepper.

- Continue to stir fry everything for 6 more mins then combine in the vermouth, tomato, and pasta.
- Stir the mix and cook everything for 3 mins.
- Top the pasta mix with the pepper flakes, cheese, and parsley.
- Enjoy.

Amount per serving: 6

Timing Information:

| Preparation | 15 mins |
| Total Time | 35 mins |

Nutritional Information:

Calories	155.8
Fat	2.1g
Cholesterol	4.4mg
Sodium	98.0mg
Carbohydrates	27.7g
Protein	7.0g

* Percent Daily Values are based on a 2,000 calorie diet.

Winter Solstice Gazpacho

Ingredients

- 2 1/2 C. water, for blending
- 1 slice day-old white bread, crusts removed, torn into pieces
- 2 oz. blanched almonds
- 2 garlic cloves, fresh, skinned, roughly chopped
- 1 tbsp olive oil
- 1 tbsp white wine vinegar
- 1 tsp salt
- 2 1/2 C. water, for diluting
- 1 bunch white grapes, small

Directions

- Add the following to the bowl of a food processor: water, white bread, almonds, cloves, olive oil, and vinegar.
- Puree the mx until you have a smooth thick liquid then add a bit more salt and vinegar if you like.
- Place the mix in a bowl and place a covering of plastic on the bowl.
- Put everything in the fridge for 60 mins until it is cold then divide the gazpacho between serving dishes.
- Serve with some grapes.
- Enjoy.

Amount per serving: 4

Timing Information:

| Preparation | 20 mins |
| Total Time | 1 hr 20 mins |

Nutritional Information:

Calories	200.6
Fat	11.3g
Cholesterol	0.0mg
Sodium	636.2mg
Carbohydrates	23.6g
Protein	4.5g

* Percent Daily Values are based on a 2,000 calorie diet.

Gazpacho Medley

Ingredients

- 2 lbs ripe tomatoes, peeled, seeded, and coarsely chopped
- 1 medium sweet onion, coarsely chopped
- 1 large cucumber, peeled and coarsely chopped
- 1/2 green bell pepper, coarsely chopped
- 1/2 red bell pepper, coarsely chopped
- 2 scallions, coarsely chopped
- 3 garlic cloves
- 1/3 C. extra virgin olive oil
- 3 tbsps sherry wine vinegar or 3 tbsps balsamic vinegar
- 1 -2 tsp hot pepper sauce
- 1 tsp ground cumin
- 1/2-1 C. chilled tomato juice
- salt & freshly ground black pepper, to taste
- Garnishes
- croutons or chopped fresh herbs or sliced scallions or diced avocado

Directions

- Get a bowl, combine: garlic, tomatoes, scallions, onion, bell peppers, and cucumbers.

- Place half of the mix into a food processor and puree everything then add in the rest and continue to puree the mix.
- Place everything back into the bowl and combine in the cumin, olive oil, hot sauce, and vinegar.
- Stir the mix then add in the tomato juice and continue to stir.
- Keep an eye on the amount of tomato mix you are adding, try to find a consistency that you enjoy.
- Add in some black pepper and salt and stir the mix again.
- Place a covering of plastic on the bowl and place everything in the fridge for 2 hours.
- Now stir the mix and divide everything between serving bowls and add in some diced avocado, croutons, scallions, and herbs.
- Enjoy.

Amount per serving: 6

Timing Information:

Preparation	15 mins
Total Time	15 mins

Nutritional Information:

Calories	161.8
Fat	12.5g
Cholesterol	0.0mg
Sodium	87.0mg
Carbohydrates	12.3g
Protein	2.4g

* Percent Daily Values are based on a 2,000 calorie diet.

Ginger Gazpacho

Ingredients

- 3 large very ripe tomatoes, cored, seeded, and cut up
- 2 medium cucumbers, seeded and cut up
- 2 medium orange sweet bell pepper, seeded and cut up
- 1 jalapeno, seeded and cut up
- 1 garlic clove, diced
- 1/3 C. lime juice
- 2 tbsps honey
- 2 tbsps fresh cilantro leaves
- 1 1/2 tsps grated fresh ginger
- 1/4 tsp sea salt
- ice cube
- lime wedges and green onion
- v-8 juice (optional)

Directions

- Get a bowl, mix: garlic, tomatoes, sweet pepper, and cucumber.
- Add half of the mix to the bowl of a food processor and puree the mix until it is chunky then add in the rest of the mix and puree everything again.

- Combine in 1/4 C. of sea salt, lime juice, ginger, cilantro, and honey.
- Puree everything until it is smooth.
- Add two pieces of ice to your serving dish and top the ice with an even amount of gazpacho.
- Garnish the gazpacho with the green onions and some lime pieces.
- Enjoy.

Amount per serving: 4

Timing Information:

Preparation	20 mins
Total Time	20 mins

Nutritional Information:

Calories	104.2
Fat	0.7g
Cholesterol	0.0mg
Sodium	161.1mg
Carbohydrates	25.6g
Protein	3.1g

* Percent Daily Values are based on a 2,000 calorie diet.

Hot Gazpacho

Ingredients

- 3 tbsps extra virgin olive oil
- 3/4 C. chopped red onion
- 3/4 C. chopped red bell pepper
- 3/4 C. chopped green bell pepper
- 3 large garlic cloves, diced
- 2 C. organic tomato juice
- 2 C. spicy vegetable juice
- 1 C. Clamato juice
- 1 C. organic chicken broth
- 3 tbsps parsley
- 3 tbsps basil
- 3 tbsps chives
- kosher sea salt & freshly ground black pepper
- 2 C. seeded diced fresh tomatoes
- 1 cucumbers, diced

Directions

- Begin to stir fry your garlic, onion, and bell peppers for 10 mins.
- Then combine in the chives, tomato juice, basil, v-8, chicken broth, and clamato.
- Stir the mix then add in some black pepper and salt.

- Get everything boiling then shut the heat and combine in the cucumber and tomatoes.
- Stir the mix again then place the gazpacho in a bowl and place a covering of plastic on the bowl.
- Put everything in the fridge for 8 hrs.
- Now stir the gazpacho again and divide the mix between serving dishes.
- Top each dish with croutons and cheese.
- Enjoy.

Amount per serving: 8

Timing Information:

| Preparation | 15 mins |
| Total Time | 25 mins |

Nutritional Information:

Calories	115.4
Fat	5.6g
Cholesterol	0.0mg
Sodium	536.8mg
Carbohydrates	15.5g
Protein	2.8g

* Percent Daily Values are based on a 2,000 calorie diet.

South American Gazpacho

Ingredients

- 2 lbs tomatoes, stems removed, cleaned
- 1 garlic clove, peeled
- 1/2 an onion, white, diced and peeled
- 1 green sweet pepper, rinsed, diced, seed removed
- 1 cucumber, about 6-7 inches long, peeled
- 1/4 tsp ground cumin
- 3 tbsps red wine vinegar
- 1/2 tbsp salt
- 1 C. virgin olive oil
- 1 piece French bread

Directions

- Let your bread sit submerged in water for 5 mins then remove the liquids and squeeze the bread to drain more water from it.
- Add the following to the bowl of a food processor: moist bread, tomatoes, cucumber, garlic, pepper, and onions.
- Pulse the mix until everything is smooth and all the pieces are small, then add in the cumin, vinegar, salt, French bread (broken into pieces), and olive oil.
- Pulse everything again until it is creamy.

- Place everything in a bowl and put the mix in the fridge until it is chilled.
- Enjoy.

Amount per serving: 6

Timing Information:

| Preparation | 10 mins |
| Total Time | 15 mins |

Nutritional Information:

Calories	378.5
Fat	36.5g
Cholesterol	0.0mg
Sodium	619.8mg
Carbohydrates	12.7g
Protein	2.6g

* Percent Daily Values are based on a 2,000 calorie diet.

Garlic Crouton Gazpacho

Ingredients

- 2 red bell peppers, seeded and coarsely chopped
- 1 cucumber, peeled, seeded, and coarsely chopped
- 14 oz. tomatoes, large and juicy ones, skinned, seeded and coarsely chopped
- 4 tbsps olive oil
- 2 tbsps sherry wine vinegar
- salt and pepper
- Garlic Croutons
- 2 tbsps olive oil
- 1 garlic clove, halved
- 2 slices bread, crusts removed and cut into 1/4 inch cubes
- sea salt
- diced green and red bell pepper
- chopped seeded cucumber
- chopped scallion
- ice cube

Directions

- Add the following to the bowl of a food processor: vinegar, bell peppers, olive oil, tomatoes, and cucumbers.
- Puree the mix then add in some pepper and salt.

- Place everything in a bowl and place a covering of plastic on the bowl.
- Place it all in the fridge for 5 hrs.
- At the same time begin to stir fry your garlic in oil for 3 mins then remove the garlic from the oil and add in the pieces of bread.
- Fry the bread until is gold all over then place the pieces on some paper towel to drain.
- Top the bread with some sea salt and place the pieces in a container.
- Once the gazpacho is chilled get your bowls for serving and add 2 ice cubes to each one and evenly divide your gazpacho between the bowls.
- Top everything with the croutons.
- Enjoy.

Amount per serving: 4

Timing Information:

Preparation	15 mins
Total Time	30 mins

Nutritional Information:

Calories	261.1
Fat	21.1g
Cholesterol	0.0mg
Sodium	73.2mg
Carbohydrates	16.7g
Protein	2.9g

* Percent Daily Values are based on a 2,000 calorie diet.

Classical Gazpacho

Ingredients

- 4 C. tomato juice
- 1 onion, diced
- 1 green bell pepper, diced
- 1 cucumber, chopped
- 2 C. chopped tomatoes
- 2 green onions, chopped
- 1 clove garlic, diced
- 3 tbsps fresh lemon juice
- 2 tbsps red wine vinegar
- 1 tsp dried tarragon
- 1 tsp dried basil
- 1/4 C. chopped fresh parsley
- 1 tsp white sugar
- salt and pepper to taste

Directions

- Add the following to the bowl of a food processor: black pepper, tomato juice, salt, onion, sugar, bell peppers, parsley, cucumber, basil, tomatoes, tarragon, green onions, wine vinegar, lemon juice, and garlic.
- Stir the mix evenly then place everything into a bowl and place a covering of plastic on the bowl.
- Put everything in the fridge for 3 hrs. Enjoy.

Amount per serving (10 total)

Timing Information:

Preparation	
Cooking	20 m
Total Time	2 h 20 m

Nutritional Information:

Calories	39 kcal
Fat	0.2 g
Carbohydrates	< 9.2g
Protein	1.6 g
Cholesterol	0 mg
Sodium	305 mg

* Percent Daily Values are based on a 2,000 calorie diet.

Verde Gazpacho

Ingredients

- 2 C. diced honeydew melon
- 1 English (seedless) cucumber, peeled and diced
- 1 small onion, diced
- 1 avocado - peeled, pitted, and chopped
- 1 jalapeno pepper, seeded and coarsely chopped
- 1 clove garlic, chopped
- 1/4 C. white balsamic vinegar
- 1 tbsp lime juice
- salt and freshly ground black pepper to taste

Directions

- Add the following to the bowl of a food processor and puree the mix: black pepper, honeydew, salt, cucumber, lime juice, onion, balsamic vinegar, avocado, garlic, and jalapeno.
- Puree the mix until it is smooth then add in some pepper and salt.
- Enjoy.

Amount per serving (2 total)

Timing Information:

Preparation	
Cooking	25 m
Total Time	55 m

Nutritional Information:

Calories	276 kcal
Fat	15.1 g
Carbohydrates	36.3g
Protein	5.1 g
Cholesterol	0 mg
Sodium	47 mg

* Percent Daily Values are based on a 2,000 calorie diet.

Artisan Gazpacho

Ingredients

- 64 fluid oz. tomato and clam juice cocktail
- 3 lbs cooked shrimp, peeled and deveined
- 4 avocados, peeled and chopped
- 2 cucumbers, cubed
- 3 large tomatoes, diced
- 1 red onion, diced
- 1 bunch cilantro, chopped
- 2 tbsps lemon juice
- 1/2 tsp salt
- 1/4 tsp pepper

Directions

- Get a bowl, combine: pepper, tomato, salt, clam juice, cilantro, shrimp, red onions, avocados, tomatoes, lemon juice, and cucumbers.
- Place a covering of plastic on the bowl, and put everything in the fridge until chilled.
- Enjoy.

Amount per serving (12 total)

Timing Information:

Preparation	
Cooking	20 m
Total Time	20 m

Nutritional Information:

Calories	322 kcal
Fat	11.2 g
Carbohydrates	29.1g
Protein	27.1 g
Cholesterol	221 mg
Sodium	948 mg

* Percent Daily Values are based on a 2,000 calorie diet.

Countryside Gazpacho

Ingredients

- 2 1/2 C. tomato-vegetable juice cocktail
- 2 1/2 C. vegetable broth
- 3 large tomatoes, diced
- 3 large avocados - peeled, pitted, and cut into bite-sized pieces
- 1 C. diced cucumber
- 1 (8 oz.) can chopped tomatoes with juice
- 1/2 C. chopped green bell pepper
- 1/2 C. chopped red bell pepper
- 1/4 C. extra-virgin olive oil
- 3 green onions, thinly sliced
- 1 lemon, juiced, or more to taste
- 2 tbsps diced fresh cilantro
- 2 tbsps white wine vinegar
- 1 dash hot sauce
- salt and ground black pepper to taste

Directions

- Get a bowl, combine: black pepper, tomato juice, salt, broth, hot sauce, tomatoes, avocados, vinegar, cucumber, cilantro, canned

tomatoes and liquid, lemon juice, bell peppers, green onions, and olive oil.
- Place a covering of plastic on the bowl and put everything in the fridge for 4 hrs.
- Enjoy.

Amount per serving (8 total)

Timing Information:

Preparation	
Cooking	30 m
Total Time	3 h 30 m

Nutritional Information:

Calories	287 kcal
Fat	23.1 g
Carbohydrates	21g
Protein	4.5 g
Cholesterol	0 mg
Sodium	392 mg

* Percent Daily Values are based on a 2,000 calorie diet.

Balsamic Gazpacho

Ingredients

- 6 medium ripe tomatoes, diced
- 2 cucumbers, peeled and finely chopped
- 1 onion, diced
- 1 green bell pepper, diced
- jalapeno pepper, seeded and diced
- 1 large lemon, juiced
- 1 tbsp balsamic vinegar
- 2 tsps olive oil
- 1 tsp kosher salt
- 1/2 tsp ground black pepper
- 1/4 C. chopped fresh dill

Directions

- Get a bowl, combine: jalapeno, tomatoes, bell peppers, cucumber, and onions.
- Stir the mix then add in the pepper, lemon juice, salt, balsamic and olive oil.
- Stir the mix again then add half of the mix to the bowl of a food processor and puree it then combine in the rest of the gazpacho and puree it as well.
- Enjoy.

Amount per serving (6 total)

Timing Information:

Preparation	
Cooking	25 m
Total Time	1 h 25 m

Nutritional Information:

Calories	58 kcal
Fat	2 g
Carbohydrates	10.9g
Protein	2 g
Cholesterol	0 mg
Sodium	330 mg

* Percent Daily Values are based on a 2,000 calorie diet.

Avocado and Garlic Gazpacho

Ingredients

- 2 C. shredded zucchini
- 1 onion, coarsely chopped
- 1 avocado - peeled, pitted, and coarsely chopped
- 1/2 C. canned garbanzo beans, drained
- 1/4 C. apple cider vinegar
- 1 jalapeno pepper, seeded and diced
- 2 tsps lemon juice
- 1 clove garlic, smashed
- 1/4 tsp salt, or more to taste
- 1/4 tsp ground black pepper, or more to taste

Directions

- Get a bowl, combine: black pepper, zucchini, salt, onion, garlic, avocado, garbanzo, lemon juice, apple cider, and jalapenos.
- Stir the mix then place a covering of plastic on the bowl.
- Put everything in the fridge for 60 mins.
- Enjoy.

Amount per serving (4 total)

Timing Information:

Preparation	
Cooking	20 m
Total Time	1 h 20 m

Nutritional Information:

Calories	155 kcal
Fat	7.9 g
Carbohydrates	19.4g
Protein	4 g
Cholesterol	0 mg
Sodium	248 mg

* Percent Daily Values are based on a 2,000 calorie diet.

Southern Gazpacho

Ingredients

- 5 C. shredded green cabbage
- 1/2 C. chopped cucumber
- 1 C. chopped tomato
- 1/2 C. chopped yellow bell pepper
- 1/2 C. chopped green onions
- 1/2 C. chopped celery
- 1/4 C. tomato-vegetable juice cocktail
- 1/4 C. red wine vinegar
- 1 tsp white sugar
- 1 tbsp olive oil
- 1 tbsp salsa
- 1/2 lemon, juiced
- salt and pepper to taste

Directions

- Get a bowl, combine: celery, cabbage, green onions, cucumbers, bell peppers, and tomatoes.
- Get a 2nd bowl, combine: lemon juice, tomato juice, salsa, vinegar, olive oil, and sugar.
- Stir in some pepper and salt.
- Combine both bowls then place a covering of plastic on the bowl and put everything in the fridge for 3 hrs. Enjoy.

Amount per serving (6 total)

Timing Information:

Preparation	
Cooking	20 m
Total Time	2 h 20 m

Nutritional Information:

Calories	63 kcal
Fat	2.5 g
Carbohydrates	10.6g
Protein	1.9 g
Cholesterol	0 mg
Sodium	132 mg

* Percent Daily Values are based on a 2,000 calorie diet.

Sunrise Gazpacho

Ingredients

- 3 pints hulled strawberries
- 1/2 cucumber - peeled, seeded, and chopped
- 1/2 onion, chopped
- 1/4 C. chopped fresh cilantro
- 1/4 C. chopped fresh parsley
- 1 pint hulled strawberries, chopped
- 1/2 cucumber - peeled, seeded, and chopped
- 1/2 onion, chopped
- 1/4 C. chopped fresh cilantro
- 1/4 C. chopped fresh parsley
- 1 bunch green onions, diced
- 1 jalapeno pepper, seeded and diced
- 1/3 C. red wine vinegar
- 3 tbsps fresh lemon juice
- 2 tbsps olive oil
- 1 1/2 tsps salt
- 2 cloves garlic, diced
- 1 tsp dried tarragon
- 1 tsp dried basil
- 1/4 tsp hot pepper sauce
- 1/8 tsp ground black pepper
- 1 large avocado - peeled, pitted, and cubed

Directions

- Add the following to the bowl of a food processor: 1/4 C. parsley, 3 pints strawberries, 1/4 C. cilantro, half of the onion, half of the cucumber.
- Process the mix for 1 min then place everything in a bowl.
- Now add the following to the pureed mix: black pepper, 1 pint strawberries, hot sauce, 1/2 cucumber, basil, tarragon, 1/2 onion, garlic, salt, 1/4 C. cilantro, olive oil, 1/4 C. parsley, lemon juice, wine vinegar, jalapenos, and green onions.
- Top everything with the pieces of avocado then place a covering of plastic on the bowl and put the mix in the fridge for 3 hrs.
- Enjoy.

Amount per serving (6 total)

Timing Information:

Preparation	
Cooking	30 m
Total Time	2 h 30 m

Nutritional Information:

Calories	231 kcal
Fat	12.4 g
Carbohydrates	31.4g
Protein	4.2 g
Cholesterol	0 mg
Sodium	605 mg

* Percent Daily Values are based on a 2,000 calorie diet.

Lime Gazpacho

Ingredients

- 2 C. 1/4-inch-diced fresh mangoes
- 2 C. orange juice
- 2 tbsps extra-virgin olive oil
- 1 seedless cucumber, cut into 1/4-inch dice
- 1 small red bell pepper, seeded and cut into 1/4-inch dice
- 1 small onion, cut into 1/4-inch dice
- 2 medium garlic cloves, diced
- 1 small jalapeno pepper, seeded and diced (optional)
- 3 tbsps fresh lime juice
- 2 tbsps chopped fresh parsley, basil or cilantro
- Salt and freshly ground black pepper

Directions

- Add the oil, orange juice, and mangoes to the bowl of a food processor and puree the mix.
- Place everything in a bowl then add in some pepper and salt.

- Place a covering of plastic on the bowl and put everything in the fridge for 60 mins.
- Enjoy.

Parsley Gazpacho

Ingredients

- 1 (1 lb) package bacon, cut into 1-inch pieces
- 8 large ripe tomatoes, diced
- 1/2 salad cucumber, diced
- 1 onion, chopped
- 1 tbsp extra-virgin olive oil
- 1 clove garlic, diced
- 1/4 tsp dried parsley, or to taste
- salt and ground black pepper to taste

Directions

- Stir fry your bacon for 12 mins until fully done then place the bacon to the side and crumble it.
- Add the onion, cucumber, and tomatoes to a bowl of a food processor and puree the mix.
- Now begin to stir fry your garlic for 60 mins in olive oil then add the pureed mix to the oil.
- Stir everything then add in the pepper, salt, and parsley and stir everything again.

- Place a lid on the pan, set the heat to low, and let the contents cook for 1 hr.
- Top the gazpacho with the bacon.
- Enjoy.

Amount per serving (6 total)

Timing Information:

Preparation	20 m
Cooking	50 m
Total Time	1 h 10 m

Nutritional Information:

Calories	210 kcal
Fat	13.2 g
Carbohydrates	12.6g
Protein	11.7 g
Cholesterol	27 mg
Sodium	587 mg

* Percent Daily Values are based on a 2,000 calorie diet.

Maggie's Favorite Gazpacho

Ingredients

- 8 C. cold water
- 8 large tomatoes - peeled, seeded and chopped
- 1/4 C. diced onion
- 1 clove garlic, diced
- 1 cucumber, peeled and finely chopped
- 1 green bell pepper, diced
- 1 (1 lb) loaf stale French bread, cut into 1 inch cubes
- 1/4 C. olive oil
- 1/4 C. wine vinegar
- 1/8 tbsp salt

Directions

- Add the following to a big pot: oil, water, bread, and tomatoes.
- Add the green pepper, onions, cucumbers, and garlic to the bowl of a food processor and puree the mix.
- Add the puree to the pot. With a hand blender, blend the mix until it is smooth, then combine in some salt and the vinegar.
- Enjoy.

Amount per serving (7 total)

Timing Information:

Preparation	10 m
Cooking	1 h
Total Time	1 h 10 m

Nutritional Information:

Calories	301 kcal
Fat	9.4 g
Carbohydrates	46.5g
Protein	9.8 g
Cholesterol	0 mg
Sodium	553 mg

* Percent Daily Values are based on a 2,000 calorie diet.

Orange and Watermelon Gazpacho

Ingredients

- 2 C. 1/4-inch-diced watermelon
- 2 C. orange juice
- 2 tbsps extra-virgin olive oil
- 1 seedless cucumber, cut into 1/4-inch dice
- 1 small yellow bell pepper, seeded and cut into 1/4-inch dice
- 1 small onion, cut into 1/4-inch dice
- 2 medium garlic cloves, diced
- 1 small jalapeno pepper, seeded and diced (optional)
- 3 tbsps fresh lime juice
- 2 tbsps chopped fresh parsley, basil or cilantro
- Salt and freshly ground black pepper

Directions

- Pure the oil, orange juice, and watermelon until smooth then place everything in a bowl.
- Add in the cucumbers, bell peppers, onion, garlic, jalapenos, lime juice, parsley, and some pepper and salt.

- Stir the mix then place a covering of plastic on the bowl.
- Put everything in the fridge until it is chilled.
- Enjoy.

Amount per serving (6 total)

Timing Information:

Preparation	10 m
Cooking	1 h
Total Time	1 h 10 m

Nutritional Information:

Calories	110 kcal
Fat	4.8 g
Carbohydrates	16.4g
Protein	1.8 g
Cholesterol	0 mg
Sodium	3 mg

* Percent Daily Values are based on a 2,000 calorie diet.

Hawaiian Gazpacho

Ingredients

- 2 C. fresh pineapple in 1/4-inch dice
- 2 C. pineapple juice
- 2 tbsps extra virgin olive oil
- 1 seedless cucumber, cut into 1/4-inch dice
- 1 small red bell pepper, seeded and cut into 1/4-inch dice
- 1 small onion, cut into 1/4-inch dice
- 2 medium garlic cloves, diced
- 1 small jalapeno pepper, seeded and diced (optional)
- 3 tbsps fresh lime juice
- 2 tbsps chopped fresh parsley, basil or cilantro
- Salt and freshly ground black pepper

Directions

- Puree the oil and half a C. of pineapple with liquid until smooth then place the mix in a bowl.
- Add the rest of the pineapple, the fresh pineapple, cucumber, bell peppers, onion, garlic, jalapenos, lime juice, parsley, some black pepper, and salt.

- Stir the mix then place a covering of plastic on the bowl.
- Put everything in the fridge until chilled.
- Enjoy.

Amount per serving (6 total)

Timing Information:

Preparation	10 m
Cooking	1 h
Total Time	1 h 10 m

Nutritional Information:

Calories	130 kcal
Fat	4.8 g
Carbohydrates	22.2g
Protein	1.2 g
Cholesterol	0 mg
Sodium	5 mg

* Percent Daily Values are based on a 2,000 calorie diet.

Gazpacho from Spain

Ingredients

- 1 cucumber, peeled and diced
- 1 green bell pepper, diced
- 5 green onions, chopped
- 2 cloves garlic, diced
- 3 tomatoes, diced
- 2 stalks celery, diced
- 2 1/2 C. navy beans, rinsed and drained
- 2 tbsps olive oil
- 6 tbsps red wine vinegar
- 1 (46 fluid oz.) can tomato juice
- 1 tsp ground cumin
- 1 tbsp diced fresh parsley
- 1 tbsp diced fresh basil
- 1/2 tbsp diced fresh oregano
- 1/4 tsp salt

Directions

- Get a bowl, combine: tomato juice, salt, cumin, oregano, basil, parsley, cucumber, vinegar, bell peppers, olive oil, green onions, navy beans, garlic, celery, and tomatoes.
- Stir the mix then place a covering of plastic on the bowl.
- Put everything in the fridge 5 hrs. Enjoy.

Amount per serving (10 total)

Timing Information:

Preparation	
Cooking	30 m
Total Time	4 h 30 m

Nutritional Information:

Calories	140 kcal
Fat	3.3 g
Carbohydrates	23.1g
Protein	6.7 g
Cholesterol	0 mg
Sodium	709 mg

* Percent Daily Values are based on a 2,000 calorie diet.

Jalapeno Gazpacho

Ingredients

- 2 (14.5 oz.) cans diced tomatoes
- 1/2 C. water
- 2 tbsps extra-virgin olive oil
- 1 seedless cucumber, cut into 1/4-inch dice
- 1 small yellow bell pepper, seeded and cut into 1/4-inch dice
- 1 small onion, cut into 1/4-inch dice
- 2 medium garlic cloves, diced
- 1 small jalapeno pepper, seeded and diced (optional)
- 2 tbsps sherry vinegar
- 2 tbsps chopped fresh parsley, basil or cilantro
- Salt and freshly ground black pepper

Directions

- Puree the oil, water, and half a C. of tomatoes until smooth then place the mix in bowl.
- Add in the cucumber, bell peppers, onions, the rest of the tomatoes, garlic, jalapeno, vinegar, parsley, some pepper and salt.

- Stir the mix then place a covering of plastic on the bowl and put everything in the fridge for 60 mins.
- Enjoy.

Amount per serving (6 total)

Timing Information:

Preparation	10 m
Cooking	1 h 10 m
Total Time	1 h 20 m

Nutritional Information:

Calories	85 kcal
Fat	4.6 g
Carbohydrates	8.1g
Protein	1.7 g
Cholesterol	0 mg
Sodium	215 mg

* Percent Daily Values are based on a 2,000 calorie diet.

Summer Solstice Gazpacho

Ingredients

- 1 (24 oz.) jar Tomato and Basil Sauce
- 24 oz. water
- 3 tbsps fresh lemon juice
- 2 tbsps granulated sugar
- Hot pepper sauce, to taste
- 1 tbsp extra-virgin olive oil
- 1 medium fresh tomato, chopped
- 1/2 C. chopped red bell pepper
- 1/2 C. chopped yellow bell pepper
- 1/4 C. diced red onion
- 1 1/2 C. diced English cucumber
- 1/4 C. chopped fresh basil
- Salt and freshly ground black pepper, to taste
- Fresh chopped parsley, for garnish (optional)

Directions

- Get a bowl, mix: olive oil, tomato sauce, hot sauce, water, sugar, and lemon juice.
- Combine in the cucumber, tomato, red onion, and bell peppers.
- Stir the mix then add in some pepper, salt, and the basil.

- Place a covering of plastic on the bowl and put everything in the fridge for 4 hrs.
- Enjoy.

Amount per serving (4 total)

Timing Information:

Preparation	
Cooking	15 m
Total Time	3 h 15 m

Nutritional Information:

Calories	166 kcal
Fat	4.9 g
Carbohydrates	27.9g
Protein	4.2 g
Cholesterol	0 mg
Sodium	476 mg

* Percent Daily Values are based on a 2,000 calorie diet.

Crab Gazpacho

Ingredients

- 1 (64 oz.) bottle tomato and clam juice cocktail
- 1/4 C. ketchup
- lemons, juiced
- 1 tbsp chopped fresh cilantro
- 1 large cucumber, seeded and diced
- 1/2 lb cooked small shrimp
- 4 oz. imitation crabmeat, chopped
- 1 green bell pepper, chopped (optional)
- 1 avocado - peeled, pitted, and diced
- 1 tomato, diced

Directions

- Get a bowl, combine: bell peppers, cocktail juice, tomato, crabmeat, ketchup, shrimp, lemon juice, cucumber, and cilantro.
- Stir the mix then place a covering of plastic on the bowl.
- Put everything in the fridge overnight then divide the gazpacho between serving dishes.
- Top each one with some tomato and avocado pieces.
- Enjoy.

Amount per serving (4 total)

Timing Information:

Preparation	
Cooking	30 m
Total Time	8 h 30 m

Nutritional Information:

Calories	440 kcal
Fat	8.4 g
Carbohydrates	72.8g
Protein	19.3 g
Cholesterol	116 mg
Sodium	2297 mg

* Percent Daily Values are based on a 2,000 calorie diet.

Western European Gazpacho

Ingredients

- 3/4 green bell pepper, seeded
- 1/2 cucumber, peeled and sliced
- 2 cloves garlic, chopped
- 1/2 C. olive oil
- 2 day-old crusty bread rolls, cut into thick slices
- 6 tomatoes, peeled and quartered
- 1/2 tbsp kosher salt
- 1 pinch cayenne pepper
- 1/2 tsp balsamic vinegar
- 1/4 tsp olive oil

Directions

- Add the following to the bowl of a food processor: 1/2 C. olive oil, bell peppers, garlic, and cucumber. Puree the mix then combine in the bread gradually. Continue to puree each piece of bread into the mix then add in the tomatoes slowly as well. Puree the entire mix then place everything in a bowl. Stir in the cayenne and salt then place a covering of plastic on the bowl.
- Put everything in the fridge for 60 mins then top the gazpacho with 1/4 tsp olive oil and the balsamic vinegar. Enjoy.

Amount per serving (4 total)

Timing Information:

Preparation	
Cooking	20 m
Total Time	1 h 20 m

Nutritional Information:

Calories	329 kcal
Fat	28.3 g
Carbohydrates	18.2g
Protein	3.5 g
Cholesterol	0 mg
Sodium	830 mg

* Percent Daily Values are based on a 2,000 calorie diet.

Latin Gazpacho

Ingredients

- 10 ripe tomatoes, quartered
- 1/2 red onion, diced
- 1 serrano chile pepper, seeded and diced
- 1/2 C. chopped fresh cilantro, or to taste
- 2 limes, juiced
- 3 cloves garlic, peeled
- 1 tsp red wine vinegar, or to taste
- salt to taste
- 1/4 C. extra-virgin olive oil (optional)

Directions

- Add the following to the bowl of a food processor: serrano, red onions, and tomatoes.
- Puree the mix then combine in the salt, cilantro, vinegar, garlic, and lime juice.
- Puree the mix again then add in the olive oil in a slow stream as you run the machine with a low heat.
- Puree the gazpacho until it is smooth again then place everything in a serving bowl.
- Enjoy.

Amount per serving (4 total)

Timing Information:

Preparation	
Cooking	15 m
Total Time	15 m

Nutritional Information:

Calories	197 kcal
Fat	14.7 g
Carbohydrates	16.1g
Protein	3.2 g
Cholesterol	0 mg
Sodium	19 mg

* Percent Daily Values are based on a 2,000 calorie diet.

New World Ceviche

Ingredients

- 1 (16 oz.) package cooked medium shrimp, peeled and deveined
- 2 (8 oz.) packages imitation crabmeat, cut into 1-inch pieces
- 5 tomatoes, diced
- 3 avocados, peeled and diced
- 1 English cucumber, peeled and cut into bite-size pieces
- 1 red onion, diced
- 1 bunch cilantro, chopped, or more to taste
- 4 limes, juiced
- 2 jalapeno peppers, seeded and finely diced
- 2 cloves garlic, pressed
- 1 (64 oz.) bottle tomato and clam juice cocktail
- salt and ground black pepper to taste

Directions

- Get a bowl, combine: garlic, crab, jalapeno, tomatoes, lime juice, avocados, shrimp, cilantro, cucumber, and red onions.
- Stir the mix then add in the clam juice cocktail.

- Stir the mix again then place a covering of plastic on the bowl and put everything in the fridge for 8 hrs.
- Enjoy.

Amount per serving (20 total)

Timing Information:

Preparation	
Cooking	1 h
Total Time	9 h

Nutritional Information:

Calories	152 kcal
Fat	4.9 g
Carbohydrates	19.7g
Protein	8.3 g
Cholesterol	49 mg
Sodium	597 mg

* Percent Daily Values are based on a 2,000 calorie diet.

Gazpacho Appetizer

Ingredients

- 1 C. tomatoes, chopped
- 1/4 C. red onion, chopped
- 1/2 C. green bell pepper, chopped
- 1/2 C. cucumber, chopped
- 1/4 C. Italian dressing

Directions

- Get a bowl, combine: tomatoes, red onions, bell peppers, cucumber, and Italian dressing.
- Stir the mix then place a covering of plastic on the bowl.
- Put everything in the fridge for 60 mins.
- Enjoy.

Amount per serving: 20

Timing Information:

| Preparation | 5 mins |
| Total Time | 5 mins |

Nutritional Information:

Calories	12.1
Fat	0.8g
Cholesterol	0.0mg
Sodium	49.2mg
Carbohydrates	1.1g
Protein	0.1g

* Percent Daily Values are based on a 2,000 calorie diet.

Sherry Gazpacho

Ingredients

- 1 cucumber, peeled, seeded, and chopped
- 1 large tomatoes, ripe chopped
- 1/2 C. roasted red pepper, jarred chopped
- 1 celery rib, chopped
- 1 garlic clove, diced
- 1 tbsp extra virgin olive oil
- 1/2 tbsp sherry wine vinegar
- 1 tsp lemon juice
- 1/4 tsp salt
- 1/8 tsp pepper

Directions

- Get a bowl, combine: cucumber, tomatoes, red peppers, celery, garlic, olive oil, vinegar, lemon juice, salt, and pepper.
- Stir the mix, then place a covering of plastic on the bowl.
- Put everything in the fridge for 60 mins.
- Enjoy.

Amount per serving: 4

Timing Information:

| Preparation | 20 mins |
| Total Time | 20 mins |

Nutritional Information:

Calories	55.4
Fat	3.6g
Cholesterol	0.0mg
Sodium	396.9mg
Carbohydrates	5.8g
Protein	1.1g

* Percent Daily Values are based on a 2,000 calorie diet.

Gazpacho Chiller

Ingredients

- 1 1/4 C. chopped tomatoes
- 3/4 C. coarsely chopped peeled English cucumber
- 1/4 C. chopped sweet green pepper
- 2 tbsps chopped onions
- 1 clove garlic, smashed
- 2 C. tomato juice
- 2 tbsps red wine vinegar or 2 tbsps cider vinegar
- 1/4 tsp dried dill
- 1 dash hot pepper sauce
- pepper
- alfalfa sprout

Directions

- Add the following to the bowl of a food processor: garlic, tomatoes, onion, cucumber, and green pepper. Puree the mix, then add in some pepper, some salt, the tomato juice, hot sauce, dill weed, and the vinegar. Puree the mix again then place everything in a bowl covered with plastic.
- Put the gazpacho in the fridge for 60 mins then divide the dish between serving bowls.
- Top each serving with some alfalfa. Enjoy.

Amount per serving: 6

Timing Information:

Preparation	15 mins
Total Time	15 mins

Nutritional Information:

Calories	26.8
Fat	0.1g
Cholesterol	0.0mg
Sodium	222.2mg
Carbohydrates	6.1g
Protein	1.1g

* Percent Daily Values are based on a 2,000 calorie diet.

Manhattan Gazpacho

Ingredients

- 8 plum tomatoes, diced
- 1 1/2 cucumbers, skin removed, diced
- 1 1/2 onions, skin removed, diced
- 1 1/2 bell peppers, cut into 4 pieces
- 3 garlic cloves, skin removed, diced
- 3 tbsps red wine vinegar
- 5 tbsps olive oil
- 2 1/2 tsps salt
- 1/2 tsp black pepper

Directions

- Get a bowl, combine: tomatoes, cucumbers, onions, bell peppers, and garlic.
- Stir the mix to distribute the garlic then add in the black pepper and salt.
- Stir the mix again then stir in the olive oil and vinegar.
- Combine everything evenly then place a covering of plastic on the bowl and put everything in the fridge for 25 mins.
- Enjoy.

Amount per serving: 10

Timing Information:

Preparation	30 mins
Total Time	45 mins

Nutritional Information:

Calories	88.2
Fat	7 g
Cholesterol	0.0mg
Sodium	586.2mg
Carbohydrates	6.4g
Protein	1.1g

* Percent Daily Values are based on a 2,000 calorie diet.

Green Spanish Gazpacho

Ingredients

- 1 quart water
- 4 oz. fresh spinach, washed and dried in a spinner
- 3 scallions, trimmed and roughly chopped
- 1/4 C. loosely packed fresh parsley leaves
- 4 fresh nasturtium leaves
- 3 large fresh basil leaves
- 1 cucumber, roughly chopped
- 1 tbsp extra virgin olive oil
- 1 large garlic clove, chopped
- 2 tbsps fresh lime juice
- 1 1/2 C. vegetable stock
- 1/4 tsp salt
- fresh ground black pepper
- 1 scallion, white and green parts, diced
- 1 cucumber, finely diced
- thin slices lime

Directions

- Get 2 pieces of diced scallion boiling with the spinach for 2 mins then remove all the liquids.
- Place everything in the blender besides the cucumber, remaining scallions, and pepper and salt.

- Puree the rest of the ingredients then add in the cucumber and remaining scallions.
- Puree the mix again then place everything in a bowl.
- Place a covering of plastic on the bowl and put the mix in the fridge for 2 hrs.
- Enjoy.

Amount per serving: 4

Timing Information:

| Preparation | 20 mins |
| Total Time | 21 mins |

Nutritional Information:

Calories	69.0
Fat	3.7g
Cholesterol	0.0mg
Sodium	182.6mg
Carbohydrates	8.8g
Protein	2.3g

* Percent Daily Values are based on a 2,000 calorie diet.

Pasta Gazpacho

Ingredients

- 4 oz. uncooked macaroni
- 2 1/2 C. tomatoes, seeded and chopped
- 1 C. red onion, diced
- 1 C. cucumber, diced
- 1/2 C. celery, diced
- 1/2 C. green bell pepper, diced
- 1/2 C. red bell pepper, diced
- 2 tbsps black olives, diced
- 3 tbsps cider vinegar
- 1 bay leaf
- 2 tbsps fresh parsley, diced
- 1 tbsp fresh thyme, diced
- 1 garlic clove, diced
- 3 -4 dashes hot pepper sauce
- 1/4 tsp ground black pepper
- whole olive
- sliced cucumber
- dill sprigs

Directions

- Get your pasta boiling in water and salt for 9 mins then remove all the liquids.
- Get a bowl and mix the pasta with all the ingredients.

- Place a covering of plastic on the bowl and put the gazpacho in the fridge for 5 hrs.
- Add in any garnishes.
- Enjoy.

Amount per serving: 6

Timing Information:

Preparation	20 mins
Total Time	30 mins

Nutritional Information:

Calories	111.6
Fat	0.8g
Cholesterol	0.0mg
Sodium	39.5mg
Carbohydrates	22.4g
Protein	3.9g

* Percent Daily Values are based on a 2,000 calorie diet.

Ripe Gazpacho

Ingredients

- 4 ripe tomatoes
- 2 small eggplants or 1 medium eggplant, peeled and cut into large chunks
- 4 small zucchini or 2 medium zucchini, but into large chunks
- 2 medium onions, cut into large chunks
- 10 garlic cloves, peeled
- 1/2 C. extra virgin olive oil
- 1/2 C. sherry wine vinegar
- salt
- ground black pepper
- 4 C. water
- 4 slices stale bread, crusts removed and torn up
- crouton

Directions

- Set your oven to 400 degrees before doing anything else.
- Add the following to a casserole dish in the oven: olive oil, garlic, onions, tomatoes, zucchini, and eggplant.
- Roast everything for 35 mins then enter everything into a bowl.
- Add in the bread, vinegar, water, pepper, and salt.

- Stir the mix then place a covering of covering of plastic on the bowl and put everything in the fridge for 2 hrs.
- Now enter the contents into a food processor and puree it.
- Enjoy.

Amount per serving: 6

Timing Information:

| Preparation | 0 mins |
| Total Time | 45 mins |

Nutritional Information:

Calories	297.4
Fat	19.2g
Cholesterol	0.0mg
Sodium	134.5mg
Carbohydrates	30.0g
Protein	5.4g

* Percent Daily Values are based on a 2,000 calorie diet.

Mexican Gazpacho

Ingredients

- 7 (16 oz.) cans black beans, drained
- 2 (4 oz.) jars capers, drained
- 1 large raw yellow onion, grated
- 1 small raw yellow onion, grated
- 3 (4 oz.) jars sliced pimientos, drained, rinsed
- 3 tsps cumin
- 4 tbsps cilantro
- 3 limes, juice of
- 3 (8 oz.) cans green chilies, chopped variety
- 13 C. regular flavor V8 vegetable juice
- 6 tbsps extra virgin olive oil
- 6 tbsps Worcestershire sauce
- 1 1/2 C. garlic
- 3 tbsps balsamic vinegar
- 2 (12 oz.) jars medium heat salsa
- 1 (6 oz.) jars bottle hot salsa
- 3 large chopped cucumbers

Directions

- Divide all the ingredients between two large pots then puree them with a hand mixer for 5 mins each.
- Place everything in a big bowl and place a covering of plastic on the bowl.
- Put the mix in the fridge for 4 hrs.
- Enjoy.

Amount per serving: 12

Timing Information:

| Preparation | 30 mins |
| Total Time | 40 mins |

Nutritional Information:

Calories	473.6
Fat	8.8g
Cholesterol	0.0mg
Sodium	1609.5mg
Carbohydrates	83.0g
Protein	23.5g

* Percent Daily Values are based on a 2,000 calorie diet.

Strawberry Pineapple Gazpacho

Ingredients

- 1/2 C. diced pineapple
- 1/2 C. diced strawberry
- 1 C. sliced grapes
- 3/4 C. blueberries
- 1 C. apple juice
- 1/2 C. orange juice
- 1/4 tsp black pepper
- 1/2 orange, segmented

Directions

- Get a bowl, combine: blueberries, pineapple, grapes, and strawberries.
- Stir the mix then place a covering of plastic on the bowl.
- Put everything in the fridge until chilled, then divide the mix between serving bowls.
- Top each serving with the orange and pepper.
- Enjoy.

Amount per serving: 4

Timing Information:

| Preparation | 20 mins |
| Total Time | 25 mins |

Nutritional Information:

Calories	109.2
Fat	0.3g
Cholesterol	0.0mg
Sodium	3.6mg
Carbohydrates	27.4g
Protein	1.1g

* Percent Daily Values are based on a 2,000 calorie diet.

East Coast Gazpacho

Ingredients

- 1 C. tomato juice or 1 C. vegetable juice
- 1/2 C. fresh tomato, peeled, seeded, diced
- 3 1/4 tbsps celery, diced
- 3 1/4 tbsps cucumbers, diced
- 3 1/4 tbsps green bell peppers, diced
- 3 1/4 tbsps green onions, diced
- 1 1/4 tbsps white wine vinegar
- 3/4 tbsp extra virgin olive oil
- 1/3 large garlic clove, diced
- 3/4 tsp fresh flat-leaf parsley, diced
- 1/4 tsp salt
- 1/4 tsp Worcestershire sauce
- 1/4 tsp black pepper, freshly ground

Directions

- Get a bowl, combine: tomato juice, fresh tomato, celery, cucumbers, bell peppers, green onions, vinegar, olive oil, garlic, parsley, salt, Worcestershire, and black pepper.

- Stir the mix then place a covering of plastic on the bowl.
- Put everything in the fridge until chilled.
- Enjoy.

Amount per serving: 2

Timing Information:

Preparation	30 mins
Total Time	30 mins

Nutritional Information:

Calories	85.1
Fat	5.3g
Cholesterol	0.0mg
Sodium	639.2mg
Carbohydrates	9.6g
Protein	1.8g

* Percent Daily Values are based on a 2,000 calorie diet.

Little Tomato Gazpacho

Ingredients

- 1 (14 oz.) cans chicken broth
- 1 lb tomatillo, quartered
- 1 garlic clove, diced
- 2 tbsps extra virgin olive oil
- 2 medium avocados, finely diced
- 1 small cucumber, seeded and finely diced
- 1 red bell pepper, finely diced
- 1/4 small red onion, finely diced
- 2 tbsps fresh cilantro, chopped
- 1 tbsp fresh lime juice
- kosher salt, to taste
- fresh ground black pepper, to taste

Directions

- Get your garlic and tomatillos boiling in the broth.
- Once the mix is boiling set the heat to low, and let the contents gently cook for 3 mins.
- Now shut the heat and let everything cool.

- Once the mix is boiling use an immersion blender to puree the mix then add in the olive and puree everything again.
- Add in some pepper and salt then place everything in a bowl and place a covering of plastic on the bowl.
- Put the mix in the fridge until cold.
- Enjoy.

Amount per serving: 4

Timing Information:

| Preparation | 20 mins |
| Total Time | 25 mins |

Nutritional Information:

Calories	296.6
Fat	23.4g
Cholesterol	0.0mg
Sodium	344.8mg
Carbohydrates	21.1g
Protein	6.1g

* Percent Daily Values are based on a 2,000 calorie diet.

FRENCH STYLE GAZPACHO

Ingredients

- 4 oz. French bread, cut into 1/2-inch cubes
- olive oil flavored cooking spray
- 4 C. tomatoes, seeded and chopped
- 2 C. boneless skinless chicken breasts
- 2 C. cucumbers, seeded, chopped
- 1 C. chopped green bell pepper
- 1/2 C. chopped red bell pepper
- 1/2 C. red onion, diced
- 1/3 C. chopped fresh flat leaf parsley
- 1/2 C. V8 vegetable juice
- 1/4 C. red wine vinegar
- 1 tbsp extra virgin olive oil
- 1 tbsp water
- 3 garlic cloves, diced
- 1/2 tsp salt
- 1/8 tsp pepper

Directions

- Set your oven to 350 degrees before doing anything else.
- Toast your bread in the oven after coating them with olive oil, on a cookie sheet, for 20 mins.

- Get a bowl, combine: parsley, tomato, onion, chicken, bell peppers, and cucumbers.
- Get a 2nd bowl, combine: pepper, veggie juice, salt, vinegar, garlic, water, and olive oil.
- Combine both bowls then stir the mix.
- Add in the toasted bread and stir the mix again.
- Enjoy.

Amount per serving: 4

Timing Information:

Preparation	20 mins
Total Time	35 mins

Nutritional Information:

Calories	179.4
Fat	4.8g
Cholesterol	0.0mg
Sodium	560.4mg
Carbohydrates	31.0g
Protein	5.5g

* Percent Daily Values are based on a 2,000 calorie diet.

Cha-Cha Gazpacho

Ingredients

- 3 C. zucchini, diced
- 3 C. cucumbers, diced
- 1 1/2 C. red onions, diced
- 4 C. sweet peppers, diced
- 7 garlic cloves
- 8 C. vegetable cocktail
- 1 1/2 C. taco sauce
- 1 C. balsamic vinegar
- 1 tbsp honey
- hot sauce

Directions

- Chop all the veggies.
- Get a bowl, combine: honey, cocktail juice, balsamic, and taco sauce.
- Add in the veggies and serve the dish.
- Enjoy.

Amount per serving: 18

Timing Information:

Preparation	45 mins
Total Time	50 mins

Nutritional Information:

Calories	54.8
Fat	0.3g
Cholesterol	0.0mg
Sodium	433.8mg
Carbohydrates	12.6g
Protein	1.8g

* Percent Daily Values are based on a 2,000 calorie diet.

Louisiana Gazpacho

Ingredients

- 10 C. ripe tomatoes, peeled and diced
- 3 C. cucumbers, peeled and quartered
- 1/2 C. yellow bell pepper, diced
- 1/2 C. celery, chopped
- 3 C. tomato juice
- 5 tbsps olive oil
- 3 tbsps vinegar
- 3 tbsps garlic, diced
- 3 tbsps Tabasco sauce
- 2 tbsps lemon juice
- 2 tbsps creole seasoning

Directions

- Add the following to the bowl of a food processor: onion, tomatoes, bell peppers, and cucumbers.
- Get a bowl, and add in the pureed mix and the rest of the ingredients.
- Stir the mix then place a covering of plastic on the bowl.
- Put everything in the fridge for 2 hrs.
- Enjoy.

Amount per serving: 20

Timing Information:

Preparation	25 mins
Total Time	1 hr 25 mins

Nutritional Information:

Calories	58.8
Fat	3.6g
Cholesterol	0.0mg
Sodium	118.6mg
Carbohydrates	6.4g
Protein	1.3g

* Percent Daily Values are based on a 2,000 calorie diet.

Maiz Gazpacho

Ingredients

- 1 C. fresh corn, cooked
- 1 tomatoes, chopped and seeded
- 3 C. tomato juice
- 1 cucumber, unpeeled and diced
- 1/2 C. white onion, diced finely
- 1/2 jalapeno, seeded and diced
- 1 garlic clove, diced
- 2 tbsps fresh basil leaves, diced
- 3 tbsps fresh lime juice
- 1/2 tsp salt
- 1/4 tsp fresh ground black pepper
- basil leaves

Directions

- Get a bowl, combine: corn, tomatoes, tomato juice, cucumber, onion, jalapeno, garlic, basil, lime juice, salt, and black pepper.
- Stir the mix then garnish the gazpacho with the basil leaves before serving.
- Enjoy.

Amount per serving: 4

Timing Information:

| Preparation | 15 mins |
| Total Time | 1 hr 15 mins |

Nutritional Information:

Calories	93.9
Fat	0.0mg
Cholesterol	791.0mg
Sodium	22.2g
Carbohydrates	3.7g
Protein	3.8 g

* Percent Daily Values are based on a 2,000 calorie diet.

Thanks for Reading! Now Let's Try some Sushi and Dump Dinners....

http://bit.ly/2443TFg

To grab this **box set** simply follow the link mentioned above, or tap the book cover.

This will take you to a page where you can simply enter your email address and a PDF version of the **box set** will be emailed to you.

I hope you are ready for some serious cooking!

http://bit.ly/2443TFg

You will also receive updates about all my new books when they are free.

Also don't forget to like and subscribe on the social networks. I love meeting my readers. Links to all my profiles are below so please click and connect :)

Facebook

Twitter

Come On...
Let's Be Friends :)

I adore my readers and love connecting with them socially. Please follow the links below so we can connect on Facebook, Twitter, and Google+.

Facebook

Twitter

I also have a blog that I regularly update for my readers so check it out below.

My Blog

Can I Ask A Favour?

If you found this book interesting, or have otherwise found any benefit in it. Then may I ask that you post a review of it on Amazon? Nothing excites me more than new reviews, especially reviews which suggest new topics for writing. I do read all reviews and I always factor feedback into my newer works.

So if you are willing to take ten minutes to write what you sincerely thought about this book then please visit our Amazon page and post your opinions.

Again thank you!

INTERESTED IN OTHER EASY COOKBOOKS?

Everything is easy! Check out my Amazon Author page for more great cookbooks:

For a complete listing of all my books please see my author page.

Made in the USA
Middletown, DE
08 April 2019